UPPER CLASS
RHYMING SLANG

Paul Wheeler and Anne Broadhead
Illustrated by Amanda MacPhail

SIDGWICK & JACKSON
LONDON

Acknowledgements

The authors would like to direct particular centurion tanks[1] at D. Beard, D. and M. Brint, F. Darling and I. MacCormick.

[1] Centurion tanks = thanks

First published in Great Britain in 1985
by Sidgwick & Jackson Limited

Copyright 1985 by Anne Broadhead and Paul Wheeler

ISBN 0-283-99295-6

Printed in Great Britain by
Anchor Brendon Ltd, Tiptree, Essex
for Sidgwick & Jackson Limited
1 Tavistock Chambers, Bloomsbury Way
London WC1A 2SG

Introduction by Jonty

His first words to me were:

'Beware of furled umbrellas, Jonty!' And, quite frankly, I hadn't got a clue what he meant. Leaning against the college crest at first light on a summer morning, to the sound of a Viennese waltz, at the May Ball ending my first year as a Cambridge student, one was used to hearing that undergraduate sprawl of clever, mystifying, or simply obfuscate comments bandied around like so much rind in marmalade. But it was obvious that old College Punt (as his nickname was even in those days) was trying to tip me the wink about something or other, as he brushed his champagne glass conspiratorially against mine, spilling a drop on my cuff.

He looked into my eyes, registered in them about as much comprehension as in a couple of billiard balls, straightened up and apologized:

'I'm dreadfully sorry, old Harpers and Queen[1], but I thought I could smell a game pie[2].' My eyebrows, already indicating surprise verging on alarm, disappeared above my hairline. Punt checked a chuckle and gobbed a bit. 'Oh Gawd!' he concluded, 'what a pâté[3]!!!' And with this he melted into the night like a salmon mousse into the river.

[1]Harpers and Queen = Bean
[2]Game Pie = Spy
[3]Pâté De Foie Gras = Faux Pas

You can imagine my confusion, or probably not.

A few days later, all became clear. I went to see my prof. to collect my work for the summer vacation which I intended to spend with a casual acquaintance in a Tibetan monastery, and he was giving me the titles of essays to write about the development of the monarchy.

'Listen carefully!' he ordered, sharpening his lips and lowering his tone. 'What is your honest opinion of the validity of royal parks[4]?' He paused to hold up his sherry to the stained glass window, then looked at me with more hooks in his gaze than in the inside of a poacher's hatband.

[4]Royal Parks = Marx

'You haven't any idea what I mean, have you? But if you become a game, which is what we all want you to do, I will personally reveal to you the true meaning and import of "Upper Class Rhyming Slang".'

And that was my first approach to join Great Britain's Secret Service. I had unwittingly been tickled like a trout.

For obvious reasons I can't come out and go into all the ins and outs of the procedures for getting in and out of the Secret Service, but the time has come to make known one of its ancient and most respected codes: 'Upper Class Rhyming Slang' (or 'Dynasty of T'ang' as it's known in the concentric circle).

I must correct the assumption, since the recent interest in UCRS was generated by some loose Norfolk[5] in the Royal Enclosure at Ascot last year, that the slang developed amongst the gentry in parallel with Cockney Rhyming Slang. In fact, as was explained to me by my prof. when I was finally admitted as a 'game', UCRS was first introduced by Christopher Marlowe, that contemporary wordsmith of Wm Shakespeare, as his major contribution to Walsingham's Secret Service in the reign of Elizabeth I. Cockney Rhyming Slang, on the other hand, only came onto the English tongue much later (according to George Orwell in *Down and Out . . .*), and consequently doesn't have the pedigree. Which is to be expected.

As with Cockney Rhyming Slang, UCRS uses a phrase which rhymes with the actual word one wants to employ, the disguise being originally a code to transmit secret information to those who understood, while by-hearers stood by, unsuspecting. From Elizabethan times, the Secret Service has tended to move in aristocratic com-

[5]Norfolk Pork = Talk

3

pany, and so it was that Marlowe invented a secret language (or 's'lang.' for short) which employed apparently everyday speech of the posher breeds, while in fact communicating vital secrets.

Few people realize, for example, that C. Marlowe's celebrated play *Tamburlain the Great* originated from the dinner party at the Spanish embassy at which Marlowe was asked by his contact, disguised as an actor, 'When wilt thou tell us the title of our next tragedie, Kit?' (a coded question regarding the time of their next rendezvous).

'I can tell thee now, sirrah: "Tamburlain the Great"[6]!' Unfortunately, Marlowe was obliged to actually write the play since his publisher was present at the dinner and was not a member of the game. *Most* unfortunate, in fact, if you ask me.

Many historic comments and 'witty' anecdotes from the high and mighty have to be reviewed in the light of Upper Class Rhyming Slang: 'We are not amused' is claimed to have meant 'The bomb's been defused', for just one example.

UCRS filtered inevitably into the ordinary conversation between games over the years, and thence to their families and friends, many of whom were unaware that they were in fact employing an elite language which has often been responsible for preserving the highest security of our great Victoria[7]. Of course, in latter years, a great deal of this language was revealed by all those Dead Sea Scrolls[8].

It was much later that I realized the advice which old College Punt had been trying to slip me at that May Ball:

[6]Tamburlain the Great = Eight (o'clock)
[7]Victoria Station = Nation
[8]Dead Sea Scrolls = Moles

'So Jonty's spilling the beans about Upper Class Rhyming Slang – what a Stilton!!'

Stilton Cheese = Wheeze

'You can't trust furled umbrellas!' – fellows with curled hair are almost always Sir Walters[9]. Punt was absolutely right. Apart from anything else, there's a lot of sound commonsense in the dicta of Upper Class Rhyming Slang. . . .

At least, I *think* old Punt meant 'curled fellas'. . . .

Upper Class Rhyming Slang: As in . . .

Penny Black   Sack
'The chauffeur started ordering suits from my tailor so I had to give him the penny black.'

Coat of Arms   Charms
'Don't be taken in by his so-called coat of arms!'

Blue Blood   Mud
'She seems the type who wouldn't want to get blue blood on her wellies.'

String of Pearls   Girls
'Finish off your brandy and we'll go and rejoin the string of pearls.'

Cabin Cruiser   Boozer
'Let's slip down to the cabin cruiser for a few snorts.'

Son and Heir   Care
'He hasn't got a son and heir in the world.'

Old School Tie   Sly
'I know he was at Eton, but I still think he's terribly old school.'

Avant Garde   Hard
'Getting into Oxford is not as avant garde as you might think.'

[9]Sir Walter Raleigh = Wally

6

Doric Pillar   **Thriller**

'I like to round off a Saturday night by curling up with a decent doric pillar.'

Stiff Upper Lip   **Chip**

'He's a stiff upper lip off the old block.'

Life Peer   **Deer**

'The life peer is a protected species, of course: there was always a danger of it dying out.'

'Let's rejoin the string of pearls.'

String of Pearls = Girls

Horse Guard   Postcard
'I had a very pretty horse guard from Malta this morning.'

Deer Stalker   Corker
'This Duchess I met in Liechtenstein is a real deer stalker.'

Gucci Shoes   News
'Antonia must have lots of Gucci shoes. She just got back from
Rome.'

Epsom Salts   Faults
'If you marry Percy you have to accept him, Epsom salts and all.'

Sense of Occasion   Invasion
'The wonderful thing is that the British Isles haven't had a sense
of occasion for centuries.'

Havana Cigar   Pa
'If you want to get in with her you've got to get on the right side
of her Havana Cigar.'

Lord of the Manor   Spanner
'Claude was helpless when the Rolls broke down, of course: he
doesn't know one end of a lord of the manor from the other.'

Oak Chest   Underdressed
'As ever, Fenella was absurdly oak chest for the occasion.'

BUPA   Stupor
'Having passed the entire evening gargling medicinal tinctures,
Norman had long since declined into a shameless BUPA.'

Gargoyle   Boil
'Willie! Stop playing with that gargoyle on your nose – you'll
only make it worse!'

Percy's First Visit to 'The Gables'

Well, some chaps have all the Donald[1], and I thank my vintage cars[2] I'm one of them. At the Oxfam luncheon last month I met scrumptious Fenella! Oh! Fabergé Fenella! So fresh and yet so fervent! Gosh, I say, that's not bad! I must put it into the ode I'm writing to her. Anyway, as soon as I saw her, I knew she came from the right kind of grandfather clock[3]: that upright posture, determined jaw . . . and yet chatting so freely with every Sir Tom, Sir Dick and Harry in the place. Naturally I joined her admiring entourage. At closer quarters I could savour her pure white pearls and soft pink silks. Well, when she tossed a suggestion around my way about spending a weekend at her grumps, I jumped at it. Funnily enough, none of the other chaps said anything, in fact the rest slipped off – but no doubt they wanted to attend the Normandy beaches[4] in the other hall.

So you see that's how I came to be at 'The Gables' for the weekend. I was greeted on arrival by Fenella's ma, one of those sympatico old Richard the Thirds[5] one feels one could always turn to in one's hour of deadly weed[6].

[1]Donald Duck = Luck
[2]Vintage Cars = Lucky Stars
[3]Grandfather Clock = Stock
[4]Normandy Beaches = Speeches
[5]Richard the Third = Bird
[6]Deadly Weed = Need

She is obviously preoccupied with the running of family affairs, mothering her chicks and keeping them under her signet[7], for indeed she seemed to have momentarily forgotten who I was or even that I was due to arrive. She seems to have been left in charge by 'The Brigadier', but just who or what or where he is I haven't been able to find out. After dinner I noticed her pour the left-over Sauvignon back into the bottle: now that's the sort of thrift that an Oxfam official like me really appreciates.

But, my Dior, I do feel jolly concerned about the way she displays the family jewels so freely about her dignified person. I mean, one never knows – what with all these orientals[8] around these days. I shall make a point of having a word in her chandelier[9] about that at some point; such a generous soul is easy pickings for the lower breeds.

Fenella's older brother Jonty came down for the weekend too. He's everything I'd expected. I understand he's doing some frightfully hush-hush research up in Cambridge: he muttered something about elderflowers[10], but I didn't really follow. He's the model of sartorial elegance: Eiffel Tower[11] in his buttonhole; patent shoes which shine right up his trouser leg; cravat of deepest purple, reminiscent of the pope's, tied in a jaunty manner.

His cobalt blue eyes seem to winkle out one's real tennis courts[12] like an escargot from its death knell[13]. He has

[7]Signet Ring = Wing
[8]Oriental Rugs = Thugs
[9]Chandelier = Ear
[10]Elderflower = Power
[11]Eiffel Tower = Flower
[12]Real Tennis Courts = Secret Thoughts
[13]Death Knell = Shell

an enthralling grasp of the English tongue: I was so enraptured by the music of his humming-birds[14] that I confess I lost the drift of their meaning.

I am intrigued by his recollections of his Little Red Riding Hood[15] with Fenella. Did she really Ross-on-Wye[16] when she lost at croquet? Did she really throw Fortnum's[17] whenever she didn't get her own way? If she did, I'm sure it was really just her plucky spirit.

That brings me to Little Willy, or 'Willy Nilly' as he's affectionately called. He's the vintage port[18] of the family. He's terribly amusing – into every Swiss Bank[19] – no

[14]Humming-Birds = Words
[15]Little Red Riding Hood ≠ Childhood
[16]Ross-on-Wye = Cry
[17]Fortnum's = Tantrums
[18]Vintage Port = Afterthought
[19]Swiss Bank = Prank

one is safe, except perhaps Jonty who is obviously trying to impose some sort of nitro-glycerine[20] on him since he was sent down from school for creating a Brighton Belle[21] in the chemistry lab. If you ask me, it should be this Brigadier that takes Willy in hand! I really don't understand why the Brig leaves all family matters to the gels. Every time I try to talk about the Brig, however, they all say, 'Let's sail on to sunnier tropics[22], shall we. . . ?' Ah well.

Jonty very kindly drove me to the station first thing on Monday morning. But it was Fenella's response to my parting gift which will stay with me for ever. What a charming compliment to be called a 'crêpe Suzette'[23]!

People

Wm Shakespeare   Beer
'There's one thing I can say for playing in the first fifteen: it taught me how to appreciate Shakespeare.'

Aristotle   Bottle
'It must have taken a lot of Aristotle to challenge the Brigadier over the tiddlywinks game.'

Mona Lisa   Freezer
'When Ma finds out that Willy's raided the Mona Lisa, she'll wipe that smile off his face.'

Robbie Burns   Turns
'It was the Hogmanay party which brought on one of the Brigadier's Robbie Burns.'

[20]Nitro-Glycerine = Discipline
[21]Brighton Belle = Smell
[22]Tropic = Topic
[23]Crêpe Suzette = Pet

'Oh Percy! You are a crêpe Suzette!'

Crêpe Suzette = Pet

13

Michelangelo   Gigolo
'I detest that chap hanging around Ma like some Michelangelo.'

Debussy   Choosy
'Even the cat in this house is Debussy – she'll only eat oysters.'

Yehudi Menuhin   Genuine
'Is this statue Yehudi Menuhin? My God!'

Wm Wordsworth   Girth
'In middle age, one always begins to notice one's Wm
Wordsworth.'

Titian   Physician
'Oh, that looks nasty! You ought to go and see a Titian.'

Bloomsbury Set   Wet
'Don't you think it's a bit Bloomsbury to go on about unemploy-
ment – it's never bothered you!'

Mozart
'Right in the middle of the slow movement, a quiet but deadly
Mozart drifted up to the Royal box.'

Rupert Brook   Nook
'Let's take a picnic hamper down to the meadow and find a
shady Rupert.'

Marie Antoinette   Pipette
'What exactly did Little Willy do with that Marie Antoinette in
the chemistry lab?'

Cecil Beaton   Eaten
'Who's gone and Ceciled the last of the black forest gateau?'

Jesus Christ   Overpriced
'I would have bought the statue if it hadn't been Jesus Christ.'

Thomas Chippendale   Gale
'All the windows at "The Gables" need renovating. When I was
in the library I felt as if I were sitting in a Thomas Chippendale.'

'I would have bought the statue if it hadn't been Jesus Christ.'

Jesus Christ = Overpriced

Samuel Pepys   Creeps
'I really enjoyed the visit, but I must say that priest hole gave me the Sam Pepys.'

Nell Gwynne   Gin
'Jonty, we've got to do something to stop Pater going for the Nell Gwynne every night.'

Lord Byron   Iron
'Ruby, I can assure you that it is only the lower classes who no longer Lord their undergarments.'

Mountbatten   Fatten
'These eclairs are delicious, but I'm sure they're very Mountbattening.'

Princess Michael of Kent   Dent
'Terribly sorry about the Princess Michael in the Rolls, old boy!'

Louis Quatorze   Pause
'When Fenella announced her engagement to Percy, there was a pregnant Louis.'

16

A Message from India:
The Brigadier's Tale

As for the Brigadier, Upper Class Rhyming Slang was his ruin. His fateful utterance on that day in those Mars Bar caves echoes still in the poor blighter's unstable hay-wain[1], although his lips are for ever sealed.

From Calcutta to the Khyber Pass, the Brigadier's name had always been of cosmic insignificance. He was rarely required to put down his glass and come out of the club, but the incident at the Mars Bar caves turned the chicken biryani of his life into a vindaloo.

On the day of India's independence, all the Brigadier's inherited gory glory of the British Empire was to be bestowed on his Indian second-in-command – Aswas. Aswas had served his Sahib beyond the call of duty on many a state occasion and now the imminent departure of his governmental guru spurred him on to zealous anticipation of the intricate diplomacy which was to be his destiny. But alas! A spring tide comes before the coming-out ball![2]

As the Empire's rule in India drew to a close, selected Indians were initiated into all the rules of the game they were about to play, and thus the code of UCRS was

[1]Haywain = Brain
[2]Upper class proverb; vulgar equivalent = Pride Comes Before
a Fall

revealed to Aswas. But what Aswas wasn't aware of was that the Brigadier, God bless him, had never realized, in his pickled perception, the true significance of the s'lang., despite numerous futile attempts to initiate him by crack code interpreters.

So, as much as Aswas was clued up, the Brig was clueless. Muddles and mysteries followed. The most banal of instructions were seized upon by Aswas as highly significant. So, for example, the Brigadier said to Aswas one lunchtime: 'I want you personally to see that the herbaceous borders are kept properly from now on, since I'll be leaving soon.' Aswas interpreted this as a rhyming code meaning that he should carry out all subsequent secret orders. Aswas also assumed that these orders would be given, inevitably, in Upper Class Rhyming Slang. From then on, the slightest utterance of the Brig was ruminated over by the faithful Aswas to extract the secret instructions from it.

'Go and collect my new shoes!' barked the Brig one morning. Immediately, Aswas scurried round the back streets of Delhi in search of the 'latest news'. On returning, proudly waving a month-old copy of the *Times*, Aswas was most upset to find the Brigadier unimpressed and, indeed, hopping mad.

Other misunderstandings had graver effects upon the misgoverning of the whole nation. There was an outbreak of typhoid: 'Do everything possible to prevent the spread of infection!' ordered the Brig. Aswas, having duly misinterpreted this, cancelled the general election that week with alarming success.

The Brigadier's life became tormented by Aswas's earnest 'decodifying' of straightforward instructions, to the point where he could hardly bear the sight of Aswas, dreading what might happen next.

The only thing that kept the Brigadier going throughout all this was his secret cache of liquor from his still in the Mars Bar caves.

The Mars Bar caves had always been regarded locally with a mixture of superstition and dread, but little did the natives realize that now there were, indeed, 'Evil Spirits' bubbling in the bowels of those primeval hills. The Brig and Aswas made frequent sorties to the caves to check on the fermentation and replenish the stock of this 'brandy' as the Brig rather wistfully named it. Of course, Aswas lapped up any hint of cloak-and-dagger activity, and on that last fatal visit to the caves, Aswas imagined, in the intense heat, that they were involved with intrigue far more universal than the Brigadier's simple desire to get Giotto[3]. The more the Brig became tetchy (in fact with Aswas's intense scrutiny of every word and action), the more Aswas became convinced that they were on a mission of historical magnitude.

By the time they reached the foot of the hills, the Brig was so exasperated that he decided he wanted to visit his spirit alone!

'Just wait here, Aswas. I may be gone some time.'

As he waited, every permutation of order and resulting action flashed through Aswas's mind and, in this awesome place, he convinced himself that he was present at a momentous occasion.

Meanwhile, back in the caves, the Brig had discovered to his horror that his entire cache was ruined: polluted with bat-droppings. This was the final straw for the Brig. He emerged from the caves a raging Lear, tearing his hair out and red in the face, only to be confronted by the ever-eager Aswas, notebook in hand, running around him like a dog worrying a chicken, begging to know what he should do.

Thus those fatal words were spoken: 'For God's sake, just get rid of the brandy and leave me alone!!' These words were to be the last ever to pass the Brigadier's lips – so terrible was their effect.

Aswas froze in his tracks, a look of horror etched on his face. But as far as he was concerned, orders were orders.

The rest is a matter of history: in January 1948 Gandhi was assassinated.

[3]Giotto = Blotto

Names

Rolls Royce   Choice
'One pays one's money and one takes one's Rolls.'

Winnie the Pooh   Loo
'After Annabella's coming-out party, all the Winnies were completely blocked.'

Country Life   Wife
'While I'm here I'd like to pick up a diamond tiara for the country life.'

St Tropez   Gay
'I do hope going to Gordonstoun isn't going to turn Little Willie into a St Tropez.'

Leaning Tower of Piza   Visa
'Don't worry about staying on, Sheik. You can always get an extension on your Leaning Tower.'

MI5   Skive
'I don't think the Brigadier was ever in danger in India – if you ask me the whole job was just an MI5.'

Tatler and Vogue   Brogue
'I find some Tatlers completely incomprehensible.'

Burberry Skirt   Flirt
'Did you see Fenella at the Oxfam luncheon? I've never seen such a Burberry!'

Tonbridge Wells   Gels
'Jonty always seems to have steered clear of Tonbridge Wells.'

Harris Tweed   Weed
'But Fenella, he's such an appalling Harris.'

St Moritz   Fits
'Jonty can be so funny – last Christmas he had us all in St Moritz!'

'But Fenella, he's such an appalling Harris.'

Harris Tweed = Weed

Eiffel Tower   Flower
'I think that wearing an Eiffel Tower in the buttonhole some-how makes a man look bigger, don't you?'

Côte d'Azur   Manure
'The gardener assures me that a little Côte d'Azure will revitalize the roses.'

Belgravia   Saviour
'Mrs Thatcher seems to be regarded as Britain's Belgravia.'

The Hanging Gardens of Babylon   Con
'That health farm was the biggest hanging gardens I have ever come across.'

Mount Everest   Best
'Come now, Fenella, Ma knows Mt Everest.'

River Cam   Spam
'It may have been roast boar pâté but it tasted like the River Cam.'

Mont Blanc   Plonk
'To sum it up, Mt Blanc is not enough by itself to get a party off the ground.'

Pyrenees   Knees
'I wouldn't give the Porsche back to him now even if he got down on his bended Pyrenees.'

Chanel No. 5   Alive
'I'm just glad I'm Chanel!'

Sloane Square   Fair
'I don't think it's Sloane to expect me to go on a diet just as we're off to Provence for two weeks together.'

The Seasons Turn at 'The Gables' I

Spring

1 April: Letter from Fenella to Percy: '. . . Percy, my precious pomegranate, I hate to bring you down from the realms of poesy to the mundane level of the glorious dead[1], but the most ghastly fate has befallen our ancestral seat: Old Drone, the family solicitor, has told us that we have one year to pay off our private jets[2] or else . . . well, I can't bear to simper and blink[3]. Oh you, with your mind full of infinite invention: *please* can you think of a Stilton[4] to raise some elm and ash[5]? . . .'

2 April: Ma's diary: '. . . Boat race: put bet on.'

3 April: Percy to Fenella: 'My fresh Fenella! I droop and wither at the thought of your dilemma! But fear not! I have the solution: turn the gorgeous grounds of "The Gables" into an organic food garden! All your troubles will be over by the time the first dear turnip peeps above the suckling earth in a few months' time, and the profits from your tender labour will be blessed! . . .'

[1] Glorious Dead = Bread (£)
[2] Private Jets = Debts
[3] Simper and Blink = Think
[4] Stilton Cheese = Wheeze
[5] Elm and Ash = Cash

24

4 April: Fenella to Percy: 'Percy! You're a clot! I have asked about the price of turnips at Harrods, and even if we sold 100,000 it wouldn't even pay the rates! I can see now that you have as much idea about milk and honey[6] as my teddy bear! Please don't bother to contact me again until you come to your barbed wire fences[7]! . . .'

5 April: Ma's diary: '. . . Grand National: put bet on.'

10 April: Advertisement in *Homes and Gardens*: 'Arabs required to use superb country mansion called "The Gables" in Wiltshire for any (legal) – (British, Christian law, that is) – purpose. Prices reasonable, but obviously appropriate to the lifestyle to which we're accustomed. . . .'

15 April: Phone call from Ma to Jonty: 'I put an advertisement in *Homes & G.*, as you advised, but I haven't received one red setter[8] nor a single croquet ball[9]. What did I do that was Hong Kong[10]?'

20 April: The Brigadier had organized (in writing, of course) a banquet to celebrate the anniversary of D Day as a fund-raising venture. Unfortunately, all the people on his list of potential paying guests were dead.

Maundy Thursday: Ma's diary: '. . . I looked up the purpose of Maundy Thursday . . . I wonder. . . .'

[6]Milk and Honey = Money
[7]Barbed Wire Fences = Senses
[8]Red Setter = Letter
[9]Croquet Ball = Phone Call
[10]Hong Kong = Wrong

25 April: Little Willy suggests a sheep-wrestling competition for local farmers, but is ignored.

1 May: Ma's diary: '. . . Hire out lawns for cricket.'

2 May: Fenella to Percy: '. . . at least my fashion show was a Good Queen Bess[11]. A Japanese millionaire sent a *huge* order for my Easter bonnets; he works for some company called "Toyota" – I assume he knows what he's doing. . . .'

5 May: Letter from Old Drone to Ma: 'I have received a writ from a Japanese car manufacturer concerning his purchase of spare parts from Fenella: please can you advise. . . .'

Summer

3 June: Ma's diary: '. . . The Derby: get tip from stable lad. . .'

7 June: Percy to Fenella: 'I know you think I'm a beauty spot[12], but I've thought of a wizard Stilton for making a few spinning jennies[13]. Why don't you produce a bath with a built-in heater underneath – like a hot plate for food – which keeps the water warm while you soak in it? It always makes me irritated when I want to loll in the old tub but get goose-pimples after a while. I'm sure Jonty. . . .'
No reply.

[11]Good Queen Bess = Success
[12]Beauty Spot = Clot
[13]Spinning Jennies = Pennies

11 June: After considering an idea of Little Willy's, Ma puts an advertisement in the *Transatlantic Elite* journal, which appears simultaneously in New York and Florida:

'Visit a genuinely haunted Gothic mansion in Great Britain: spectres range from Poe to the Deluxe Wuthering Heights weekend: please contact "The Gables". . . .'

Friday, 13 June: The Brigadier's silent reconstruction of the Somme trenches in the dried-up moat around 'The Gables' is greeted with little enthusiasm.

15 June: Ma's diary: 'Ascot – wear last year's hat.'

21 June: Fenella's midsummer ball for the Animal Liberation Front, in which members were invited to dress up as their favourite animal, and to play inventive games such as 'Hunt the Whale' and 'Save the Seal' (in which an inflatable seal has to be kept in the air for thirty-five minutes without being touched by anything except the human head – 'consciousness raising!' she explained), attracted attention and contributions, although the vegetarian musical version of Noah's Ark, in which Noah and his family took two onions, two cauliflowers, etc. on board their boat, was unfortunately rained off.

3 July: Ma's diary: 'Queen's Garden Party – take doggy bag.'

15 July: Letter from Jonty to Ma: '. . . Don't say anything to a Wedgwood bowl[14], but I think I've cracked the way for us to get out of this financial South-east Cape[15].

[14]Wedgwood Bowl = Soul
[15]South-east Cape = Scrape

Mum's the word, but it's to do with elderflower[16] and the Dynasty of T'ang[17] . . . I'm sure you know what I mean.'

Ma is not at all sure, and worries that Jonty has come under the influence of some oriental weed.

26 July: Ma's diary: 'Goodwood: Willy can't go.'

5 August: Little Willy's Extremely Young Conservative camp in the grounds of 'The Gables' is a lucrative scheme, especially his 'quid-a-job' campaign, as is the sale, inspired by Percy, of parents' 'unwanted' and 'unnecessarily cruel' fur and leather clothes at knock-down prices.

[16]Elderflower = Power
[17]Dynasty of T'ang = Upper Class Rhyming Slang

28

12 August: Ma's diary: 'The Glorious Twelfth! – supply Harrods.'

20 August: An Arab sheik arrives, duly answering the spring advertisement in *Homes and Gardens*, to discuss the possibility of using 'The Gables' and grounds as an airport, but the Brig unfortunately mines his helicopter.

25 August: In the ice-sculpture competition organized by Fenella, the judges are unanimous in awarding first prize to Ma's self-portrait entitled *Lady with Fruit*.

Food and Drink

Claret and Port   Thought
'This book has certainly given me some food for claret and port.'

Buck's Fizz   Tizz
'What with the chauffeur, the Hunt Ball and the oysters, I was in an utter Buck's Fizz.'

After-Dinner Speech   Leech
'Viscount Jagger – always the last to leave – hangs around like an after-dinner speech.'

Brace of Pheasant   Present
'It's so difficult choosing a suitable brace of pheasant for a coronation.'

Dinner Gong   Song
'I never could understand all that Latin in the school dinner.'

Gin and Tonic   Chronic
'Well, I'm not really sure what Jonty thought about my pomes, Fenella. When I asked him he just said "gin and tonic"!'

Jugged Hare   Dare
'Rumour has it that Jonty ate sixty-nine hard-boiled quail eggs once, just for a jugged hare.'

Lemon Meringue Pie   Tie
'My God, Percy, you can't seriously be considering wearing that lemon!'

Hors d'Oeuvres   Nerve
'It must have taken Percy a lot of hors d'oeuvres to propose to Fenella.'

Picnic Hamper   Pamper
'All this talk about Oxfam has made my son Willy picnic hamper all the servants.'

Asparagus Spears   Tears
'Fenella knows that all she has to do to get her own way is to
burst into asparagus.'

Scotch on the Rocks   Socks
'There is nothing worse than a man whose cravat doesn't match
his scotch on the rocks.'

Pink Gin   Din
'You call it "Bartok", do you? Well, I'd call it a frightful pink gin!'

Jerusalem Artichoke   Joke
'Have you heard the Jerusalem about the Count, the Marquis
and the Sheik?'

Haute Cuisine   Scene
'Ma discovered Nigel and Fiona in a clinch on the chaise longue
and launched into the most frightful haute cuisine.'

Light Luncheon   Truncheon
'. . . and then this policeman hit the miner over the head with
his light luncheon.'

Dover Sole   Hole
'She looked an absolute sight with a Dover sole in her stocking.'

Royal Jelly   Belly
'Willy! It's really not done to refer to Percy's abdomen as his
"royal jelly".'

The Seasons Turn at 'The Gables' II

Autumn

1 September: Percy to Ma: 'I haven't been able to thank you before for the five mink coats which you so generously gave Willy for our sale in the summer. As social organizer for Vegan International, I was hoping that you would let us use "The Gables" for our annual "Conversations with Vegetables" rally, which is part of our harvest festival celebrations. Normally this event is chick pea[1], but I see no reason why we shouldn't make a small polyunsaturated marge[2] to help boost the family's runner beans[3]. . . .'

3 September: Ma to Percy: '. . .you have gone too Russian tzar[4]!! Kindly leave us all on the throne[5]!!'

10 September: Ma's diary: 'Burghley Horse Trials: prizes?'

13 September: The first Ghost Weekend, suitably timed for the mists and mellow fruitlessness of autumn, sees a high-school teacher and her drummer husband from

[1]Chick Pea = Free
[2]Polyunsaturated Marge = Charge
[3]Runner Beans = Means
[4]Russian Tzar = Far
[5]On the Throne = Alone

Long Island embedded in the hastily redecorated 'Wuthering Heights' wing of 'The Gables'. Although Fenella does a brave job of imitating Cathy, singing plaintively from the silver birch trees in a translucent coming-out dress left over from the fashion show, Willy is an unconvincing Heathcliff. His appearance at the window is marred by the fact that his head doesn't come up as far as the sill. An unseasonable thunderstorm rounds off the Sunday night dramatically, and although it gives Little Willy a nasty cold, it encourages the Americans to pay off and fly back to the relative calm of their homeland.

15 September: Ma's diary: 'Beaujolais Nouveau: make do with last year's.'

6 November: Letter from Lord Earworth to Ma: '. . . I'm afraid I have to complain in the most heated terms about the nature of the fireworks at the Guy Fawkes celebration at "The Gables", which the dowager and I attended. Not only did I think that £7.50 was an inflated price for a piece of black toffee, even if, as the boy who sold it to us insisted, it was antique; but the firework display seemed to have more in common with the Ritz[6] than with a colourful art form from the last-but-not-least[7]. Please could you advise me about the exact nature of the "Gables Cripples Fund" and explain how, if this charity is so in need of funding, it can afford to dress the guy on the bonfire up in a mink coat? Incidentally, who was the Harris talking to a turnip?

Yours in ire. . . .'

[6]The Ritz = The Blitz
[7]Last-But-Not-Least = Far East

25 November: Ma's diary: 'Leaves all fallen. Dismiss gardener.'

Winter

1 December: Ma's diary: 'Varsity match: put bet on.
   King's College Carol Service: sell Jonty's ticket.'

25 December: Snow has fallen on 'The Gables' like icing on a porterhouse steak[8].The Christmas tree twinkles like a Shangri-la[9] and Little Willy is x-raying the wrapped presents with a machine that he's 'borrowed' from school.

Dressed in a red overcoat, with a white muffler and a sack over his back, a lonely figure makes its way to the front door of the mansion and rings the heaven and hell[10].

Inside, Fenella, Ma, Little Willy, the silent Brigadier and a letter from Percy stare gloomily at the King's College Choir[11] and listen gloomily to the Queen's Normandy Beach[12].

The New Year, not to mention the end of the year assigned by Old Drone, was fast approaching, and the family's coach and horses[13] were as depleted as Santa's sack on Boxing Day.

'Go and see who that is at the wild boar[14]!' Ma says to Willy in a voice like yesterday's glass of Moet & Chandon.

[8]Porterhouse Steak = Cake
[9]Shangri-la = Star
[10]Heaven and Hell = Bell
[11]King's College Choir = Fire
[12]Normandy Beach = Speech
[13]Coach and Horses = Resources
[14]Wild Boar = Door

'They listen gloomily to the Queen's Normandy Beach.'

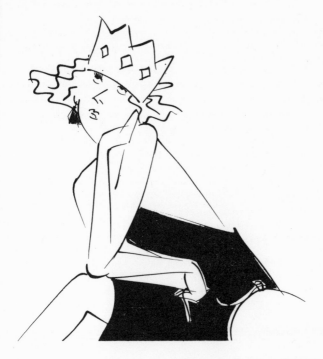

Normandy Beach = Speech

Febrile attempts to restore solvency have not been helped by the lawsuits from Japan and the damage done by the Brig's live ammunition which he detonated on 5 November.

But when the enigmatic figure from the cold casts aside his red apparel with a dazzling smile, the house lights up like Pearl Harbor: Jonty pulls from his sack a small book and a large cheque.

'It's all over! I've paid the accounts! I've sold the noblest, dearest secret ever entrusted to me, but in the process I've brought hope and joy to English-speakers, everywhere!' he announces with a flourish.

And so it is, dear reader, that you hold in your hand not merely the invigorating secret of Upper Class Rhyming Slang, but a passport for the household at 'The Gables' to live out the rest of their useless lives in peace and rhyme.

Upper Class Rhyming Slang has saved us all!

God bless every Tiny Tim[15]!!

Sport

Twelve-Bore   Law
'She saw a poacher in the grounds and simply took the twelve-bore into her own hands.'

Henley Regatta   Chatter
'Cedric tells me that Peregrine is up for an Earldom but I think that's nothing but idle Henley.'

Ascot Races   Places
'Well my dear, they're to be seen together at all the right Ascots.'

Grand Prix   Wee
'Must confess I always nip out for a Grand Prix during the Queen's speech myself.'

Hockeystick   Wick
'Oh no! you haven't invited Jeremy, have you? He really gets on my hockeystick.'

[15]Tiny Tim = Idle Whim

'She saw a poacher in the grounds and simply took the twelve-bore into her own hands.'

Twelve-Bore = Law

Three-Day Event   Gent
'Wizzie, you must meet my new boyfriend, he's so wonderful,
strong and handsome; he's a real three-day event.'

Cartridge Bag   Wag
'Make sure you invite Sidney to the Ball, he's such a cartridge
bag he'll make sure it's a hit.'

Boxing Day Meet   Treat
'Sun in the heavens, off to the river, Fenella in one hand and a
Fortnum's hamper – my idea of a Boxing Day meet.'

Hunting Horn   Dawn
'I wouldn't go to Chastity's if I were you. She's the type who
gets you up with the hunting horn and route marches you to
chapel.'

Glorious Twelfth   Health
'Frankly, I don't think it was Aswas who ruined the Brig's Glorious Twelfth, more like a few too many snifters I'd say.'

First Eleven   Heaven
'The weather in Monte Carlo was pure first eleven.'

Croquet Stick   Thick
'Lord Waddle asked me to find Algy a nook in the City, but even
playing the stock market presupposes a minimal allowance of
brains, and frankly the poor boy's pretty croquet.'

Cambridge Blue   Coup
'The Brigadier thinks that what the country needs is a Cambridge
blue.'

Leg Before Wicket   Picket
'The whole visit to Lord Barnsley's place in Yorkshire was
ruined by a leg at the gates.'

Pony Club   Snub
'Felicia has never forgiven her since that incident in the Royal
Enclosure; she thought it was a terrible pony club.'

Sporting Blue   New
'But Ma, I simply cannot go to Ascot unless I have a sporting blue hat.'

Double-Barrel Shotgun   Fun
'Tramping across the moors, green wellies glistening, tremendous double-barrel!'

Scrum Half   Bath
'I'm so sticky I simply must have a scrum half.'

Shooting Stick   Trick
'If Little Willy's got any more shooting sticks up his sleeve I'll throttle him!'

Trooping the Colour   Fuller
'Oh no Modom, I can assure you it's the latest fashion and just the thing for the trooping figure.'

Stirrup and Crop   Flop
'Do you remember the last Hunt Ball? The drink ran out at midnight; the sheep got into the marquee; it was an absolute stirrup.'

Fenella Finds a Ruby

All the family agree that 'The Gables' must seem to be maintained in immaculate condition for various reasons: not least to impress the caravans of prospective Arab buyers or the droves of American ghosthunters. To this end, the doughty Fenella has taken the reins into her own hands, and it only remains to interview the applicants for the extra staff. The arrival of Mrs Ruby Smith on the dot of 10 o'clock bodes well.

Fenella answers the ring at the door.
RUBY: 'Mornin' miss! I come about the job what I seen in the paper.'
FENELLA: 'Oh yes, do come in Mrs . . .'
RUBY: 'Mrs Ruby Smith, miss.'
FENELLA: 'We shall go up to the library first to discuss the position, then I shall show you round the house and grounds.'

They enter the library.
RUBY: 'Blimey, what a lot of apples and pears!'
FENELLA (SURPRISED): 'Do you mean you've done some research into our family's financial status?'
RUBY: 'What!? I mean ain't there a lot of stairs 'ere!'
FENELLA (LAUGHING): 'Oh, I thought you meant "apples and pears" – "shares". You see, in my circle, we have this habit of speech whereby you say one thing which rhymes with another. . . .'

RUBY: 'Exactly. So do the people round where I live – the East End – Cockney Rhyming Slang – ain't you 'eard of it?'

FENELLA: 'Good Lord! How fascinating! You mean we almost have something in common? Only your rhymes seem to be different from . . .'

RUBY: 'Well, we make our rhymes from our life – I suppose you make your rhymes from yours: "apples and pears" for "shares" – now that's something I'd never 'ave thought of. Very Porsche[1].'

FENELLA: 'Yes, well, about the position of domestic: of course, partly it involves being a Domesday Book . . .'

RUBY: 'I'll 'ave you know I come from a very honest family . . .'

FENELLA: 'I fail to see what this has to do with honesty, all I'm asking is, can you cook simple dishes or not?'

RUBY: 'Oh! Can I cook!!! Not "'ave I ever been a crook!" – oh yes, I do a very nice Kate and Sidney pie.'

FENELLA: 'Anything a trifle more adventurous – like a coq au vin?'

RUBY: 'I don't think I quite gets your drift, miss! What do you mean: "a cock in the van"?'

FENELLA: 'Oh, never mind. Now, about all the world wars. . .'

RUBY (CHUCKLING): 'The rest of the family, eh? Real old bores, are they?'

FENELLA: 'Goodness me, no. I'm referring to your "chores". We need somebody to put everything in order in the kitchen, scullery and pantry and so on. You know, put all the jam jars into the garage and so on.'

RUBY: 'Oh, sorry, miss. I can't drive.'

FENELLA: 'The garage is just next to the kitchen garden,

[1] Porsche = Posh

41

hardly far enough to warrant taking the car just to throw
out the jam jars.'

RUBY: 'Oh, I see, you *do* want me to put the jam jars out!'

FENELLA (ASIDE): 'My God, if it's going to take her this
long to understand the simplest thing, I shall be here for
ever.'

. . . 'Doubtless you noticed the extensive grounds as
you arrived, but don't worry: you won't be expected to
take care of the Brigadier's salmon and trout as well.'

RUBY: 'Oh, I wouldn't mind that. I know some natural
remedies for getting rid of salmon and trout.'

FENELLA (LOOKING AGHAST): 'Getting rid of . . . ?!'

RUBY: ''Ang on a mo' – you are talking about his gout,
ain't you?'

FENELLA: 'No, I did actually mean the salmon in the stream, and the trout farm.'

RUBY: 'Pity. I would've liked to try out my grandma's crushed kestrel's eggs remedy.'

Jonty enters the library, realizes Fenella is interviewing, goes out again.

RUBY: 'Cor blimey, who's that? Is he King Lear?'

FENELLA: 'No, no, that's my elder brother Jonty.'

RUBY: 'Still, looks like 'e's King Lear, to me.'

FENELLA: 'Now, where was I? Yes, servants do have certain bonuses; for example, you can pick up some greengages, once a year – in the summer.'

RUBY: 'I can't 'ave that, miss! Only getting me wages once a year. I mean I'm hearts of oak now.'

FENELLA: 'I mean, employees are free to take a certain amount of garden produce from the kitchen gardens and the orchards. . . . Now I'd like to show you the house and the servants' quarters.'

Fenella takes her on a guided tour of the downstairs rooms, then to her quarters.

RUBY: 'Cor, it ain't 'alf royal flush[2]! I expect you'd be able to let me 'ave a dog and bone, as it's a live-in position.'

FENELLA: 'Well, really, Mrs Smith, I do think it's a bit presumptuous to be asking for a loan already . . .'

RUBY: 'No, no – dog and bone – 'phone! To keep in touch with me family – and for phoning me jet set!'

FENELLA: 'You keep horses in Whitechapel, do you? Well, who would have thought. And which vet do you use? I always use . . .'

RUBY: 'No, no, jet set don't mean vet where I come from,

[2]Royal Flush = Plush

43

your highness, it means bet. Every week I like to put a Lady Godiva on the gee gees.'

FENELLA: 'I'm not sure we'd encourage gambling, Mrs Smith!'

RUBY: 'That's all right – I don't need no encouragement.'

FENELLA: 'Have you any other questions?'

RUBY: 'Yes, will I get to meet the real upper class in this job – you know, Torvill and Dean and that?'

FENELLA: 'I'm afraid we don't move in those kinds of circles.'

RUBY: 'No, I suppose you wouldn't really – and anyway, I suppose the Queen's got too many other royals to visit these days, what with the family growing so fast. . . .'

Homes and Gardens

Swimming Pool   Fool

'He may seem wet, but I assure you he's nobody's swimming pool.'

44

Silver Plate   Mate
'Chastity's new silver looks as though he must be worth a thou.
or two.'

Michaelmas Daisy   Crazy
'To say that the Brig was a little Michaelmas daisy would be
being too kind.'

Garden Fête   State
'How did the conservatory get into this garden fête?'

Stately Home   Poem
'I can't imagine why Percy thinks his stately homes are so
important!'

Parquet Floor   Bore
'Since she met Percy, Fenella has turned into a parquet.'

Chaise Longue   Pong
'Whatever is that chaise longue in the drawing room?'

Four-Poster Bed   Thread
'When Tristram was waffling on about rowing I completely lost
the four-poster.'

Conversation Piece   Police
'Uncle Walter seems to have attracted the attention of the conversation piece.'

Hampton Court Maze   Daze
'Since he heard the news, he's been wandering around in a
Hampton.'

Potting Shed   Bed
'One makes or breaks a marriage in a potting shed, I don't care
what they say.'

Camomile Lawn   Torn
'I'm camomile between the black taffeta and the purple satin.'

Strawberry Patch   Catch
'I'm sure Fenella's just a good strawberry as far as Percy's concerned.'

'How did the conservatory get into this garden fête?'

Garden Fête = State

46

| Window Box | Docks |

'Nothing can be done about the bird bath until the Italian marble is released from the window box.'

| Oriental Rug | Thug |

'My club in St James's just isn't the same – it's full of oriental rugs these days.'

| Servants' Quarters | Daughters |

'I told Vernon he should have locked up his servants' when that Prince came to play with his pop group.'

| Stable Lad | Cad |

'What stable lad gave Fenella's horse Guinness to drink just before the point-to-point?'

| Gamekeeper | Sleeper |

'Thank goodness the baby's turned out to be a good gamekeeper!'

| Wine Cellar | Fella |

'Who was that wine cellar you brought into the club last night?'

| Liberty Print | Squint |

'She's quite good looking apart from her Liberty.'

| Rose Garden | Pardon |

'Even if they did find out about Jonty, I expect he'd get a royal rose garden.'

Percy's Pomes

'Welcome to my stately homes.'

Stately Homes = Pomes

Apologia

Passing reader, stay awhile, and rest
thy rhyming head upon my caring breast,
Not in council flats nor pleasure domes,
But in the comfort of my stately homes[1].

Love's Blossoming

Fenella! If I've spelt it right,
Contains a vegan's rare delight!
Verdant, crisp; exotic taste –
How well Fennel reflects thy grace!

That curling hair! That pale gaze
intoxicate my salad days!
And though my Cupid's dart[2] may bleed,
Thou wilt not wilt nor run to seed!

On Our Baby Prince's First Meeting with an Aborigine

Phew! Regal Willy!
Bearing thy mother's family crest[3],
Like a tiny Windsor castle[4] in thy Royal yacht[5],
wast thou borne across the briney
Antipodean.

Oh! Royal wee one!
In this land ruled by the sun and craving the world of the
                                                    Forsyte Saga[6]!

[1]Stately Homes = Pomes
[2]Cupid's Dart = Heart
[3]Family Crest = Breast
[4]Windsor Castle = Parcel
[5]Royal Yacht = Cot
[6]Forsyte Saga = Lager

What Kings and Queens[7] can nourish thee?
Only the rude Aristotle[8] to sustain thee;
Expect no picnic hampering[9]!

But lo! What lowly creatures venture nigh?
What secret invitation beckons from the great Charles
and Di[10]?

What cuddly koala!
What kingly kangaroo!
Their Prince of Wales[11] resting, respectful;
Heads bowed before thy Verdi's Requiem[12].

But yonder! Who is this that steps from the
Charge of the Light Brigade[13]?
Is it the Prince of Darkness
Who has come to menace thee?
Why, no – it is a noble Aborigine!

Fear not! this simple Princess Anne[14]
bears no Buckingham Palace[15]:
His dingo's Captain Mark[16] is worse
Than his great Australian bite!
He offers you the best he can –
A homemade, sugared boomeringue.

[7]Kings and Queens = Beans
[8]Aristotle = Bottle
[9]Picnic Hamper = Pamper
[10]Charles and Di = Sky
[11]Prince of Wales = Tails
[12]Verdi's Requiem = Pram
[13]Charge of the Light Brigade = Shade
[14]Princess Anne = Man
[15]Buckingham Palace = Malice
[16]Captain Mark = Bark

Death Duty[17]

When I consider all my stocks and shares[18],
It seems my life's a tale of Coutts and Co[19].
The smallest national debt[20] then chills me deep in my
Dow Jones[21].

But then I let my thoughts turn to the pleasant F.T. Index[22];
And life is once more visited by infinite death duty.
First-day issues[23] vanish like the sun before capital gains[24],
And Cupid waves his government bond[25]:
I'm strong against the dollar[26].

Culture

Paddington Bear   Fare
'Go to Venice if you must, but you can take care of your own
Paddington Bear.'

Glyndebourne   Yawn
'Tea with the vicar, cricket rained off, the Duffs' latest holiday
video – quite honestly the whole weekend was an unmitigated
Glyndebourne.'

[17]Death Duty = Beauty
[18]Stocks and Shares = Cares
[19]Coutts and Co = Woe
[20]National Debt = Fret
[21]Dow Jones = Bones
[22]F.T. Index = Fair Sex
[23]First-Day Issues = Blues
[24]Capital Gains = Rains
[25]Government Bond = Magic Wand
[26]see Shakespeare: pun on 'Dollar'/'Dolour' = Grief

Last Night of the Proms   Bombs
'With these ghastly terrorist thingies around, one never knows
where the next last night of the proms will be.'

Golden Fleece   Lease
'And now the Brigadier has refused to renew the golden fleece
on the town houses.'

Lyrical Ballad   Mallard
'I think Jonty's got pluck taking a pot shot at that lyrical ballad.'

Iambic Pentameter   Amateur
'Shakespeare's a mere iambic when it comes to women.'

Viennese Waltz   False
'Pity that last race at Ascot turned out to be a Viennese start.'

Lady of Shalott   Hot
'I know I asked for devilled kidneys but I didn't expect them to
be *this* Lady of Shalott.'

Taj Mahal   Mall
'What was most unsavoury about America was all those ghastly
shopping Taj Mahals.'

String Quartet   Pet
'Good Lord no, we don't allow the servants string quartets.'

Wedgwood Blue   Flu
'There's an awful lot of Wedgwood blue around this Christmas.'

Gothic Novel   Hovel
'My dear, the way he dresses anyone would think he lived in a
Gothic novel.'

Giotto   Blotto
'And when that Landseer we found in the loft turned out to be
a Keating I marched straight round to the Laughing Cavalier
and got totally Giotto.'

'I know I asked for devilled kidneys but I didn't expect them to be *this* Lady of Shalott.'

Lady of Shalott = Hot

53

Herzog   Fog
'We'd planned to drive into town to catch the new Truffaut, but got hopelessly lost in the thickest Herzog you ever saw.'

Lady Macbeth   Death
'Ma! What's the matter? You look like Lady Macbeth warmed up!'

1812 Overture   Mature
'I don't think this port is 1812 enough to drink.'

Tiffany Lamp   Cramp
'The Queen Mother must get terrible Tiffanies every day of the week waving at every T., D. and Harry.'

Waterford Crystal   Pistol
'There's only one way to solve this – Waterfords at dawn!'

Venetian Glass   Pass
'She slapped his face because he made a Venetian glass at her at the opera.'

Paradise Lost   Cost
'We must have the west wing renovated, whatever the Paradise Lost.'

Westminster Abbey   Flabby
'What I didn't like about going to the health farm was seeing all those Westminster Abbey bodies.'

Rite of Spring   Fling
'Percy's hardly the sort of chap anyone would have a rite of spring with, is he?'

Knight of the Round Table   Cable
'If you can't get a letter through, you'll just have to send a knight of the round table.'

Upper Class Proverbs

(with vulgar equivalents in brackets where appropriate)

You can't give an old candelabra new wicks.
(*Can't teach an old dog new tricks.*)

A nouveau riche is as good as a nobody.
(*A miss is as good as a mile.*)

Every Silver Cloud has a leather lining.

A grouse in the bag is worth two at the Savoy.

Nothing invested, nothing contested.
(*Nothing ventured, nothing gained.*)

A rolling Sloane wears no Moss Bros.

A cork in time saves wine.
(*A stitch in time saves nine.*)

He who's crowned last lives longest.

Who has stocks and shares grins.
(*Who dares wins.*)

Always look a race horse in the mouth.

Enough isn't as good as a feast.

Don't feed the hand that bites you.

Red rose at night, deb's delight; red rose in the morning, deb's warning.

Beauty's only Yves St Laurent deep.

Don't put the horse box before the Range Rover.
(Don't put the cart before the horse.)

There's no class without brass.
(There's no smoke without fire.)

Upholstery of leather looks well together.
(Birds of a feather flock together.)

Blue blood is thicker than porter.

Those in flannel trousers shouldn't throw scones.
(Those who live in glass houses shouldn't throw stones.)

All at Christie's is not gold.
(All that glistens is not gold.)

You can't get blue blood out of a Sloane.

St Tropez while the sun shines.
(Make hay while the sun shines.)

In for a penthouse, in for a palace.
(In for a penny, in for a pound.)

'Spare the rod and spoil the Oscar Wilde.'

Oscar Wilde = Child

If the crown fits, wear it.

One sip doesn't make a wine cellar.
(One swallow doesn't make a summer.)

There's many a drip 'twixt goblet and lip.
(There's many a slip between cup and the lip.)

Don't count your pheasants before they're bagged.

Too many chauffeurs ruin the Rolls.
(Too many cooks spoil the broth.)

You can send a pleb. to Eton but you can't make him a Prince.
(You can take a horse to water but you can't make it drink.)

What's good for the Count is good for the Countess.

Never say Princess Di.

Many hands make little profit.
(Many hands make light work.)

Curiosity killed the aristocrat.

One royal wave doesn't make a Queen Mother.
(One swallow doesn't make a summer. q.v.)

An oyster a day keeps the gout away.

A lady's place is in the stately home.

Too many wets spoil the cabinet.

Those in flannel trousers shouldn't throw scones.'

The proof of the soufflé is in the rising.

What you lose at Ascot you gain at Monte Carlo.
(What you lose on the swings you gain on the roundabouts.)

Charles never reigns but he bores.
(It never rains but it pours.)

One man's hors d'oeuvres is another man's poisson.
(One man's meat is another man's poison.)

Quiz

1 'Jonty' is short for:
   a) Jonquil   c) Cedric
   b) Jeanne d'Arc   d) Jonathon.

2 What will Percy's next pome be about?
   a) Nancy Reagan   c) Vanessa
   b) CND   d) Duck-billed platypus.

3 Which herb or spice does Fenella remind you of?
   a) Fennel   c) Fenugreek
   b) Fennel   d) Fennel.

4 When a Brigadier loses his rank, he is:
   a) Debagged   c) Defrocked
   b) Debriefed   d) Debugged.

5 Ma once appeared on:
   a) *Desert Island Discs*   c) *The Two Ronnies*
   b) *Come Dancing*   d) *Grandstand*.

6 When Little Willy grows up he will be:
   a) Sir John Gielgud   c) The Third Ronnie
   b) A glue sniffer   d) A chartered accountant.

7   Decode the following UCRS terms:

Beef Wellington	Duchess Potatoes
Cocktail Cabinet	Chippendale Commode
Spanish Armada	Drury Lane
Shakespeare's Sonnets	Sistine Chapel
Bridle and Bit	Rhodes Scholar
Coming of Age	Ambassador Class
Okay Yah	Bowler Hat
Brighton Pier	Gilbert and Sullivan
Persian Gulf	Sherman Tank
Silver Spoon	C of E
Health Farm	

8   Substitute the correct form of UCRS, as mentioned in this book, for the words in italic in the following passage:

'You see, Jonty,' said Percy to his brother-to-be on his stag night, 'the first time I clapped eyes on that popelote of a sister of yours, I thought – now there's a *corker*!'

Although the cold light of *dawn* was on his face, Jonty looked *hot* and the outline of his knuckles showed white around the neck of the *bottle* in his hand.

'This is no time to start a *scene*, I know,' he growled, 'but as far as I'm concerned I wish to *heaven* that you'd never sent her that repulsive *poem* nor ever organized that absurd Vegans' ball. It won't just end in *bed*, you know – it'll end in *tears*.'

But Percy's *heart* was flying skyward with the *song* of the morning larks.

(This last exercise proves, in conclusion, that once you've tasted UCRS all prose without it reads like strawberries without champagne.)